The Story of Vivek

(ILLUSTRATED)

Advaita Ashrama

(Publication Department)
5 Dehi Entally Road
Kolkata 700 014

Published by
Swami Bodhasarananda
Adhyaksha, Advaita Ashrama
Mayavati, Champawat, Uttarakhand, Himalayas
from its Publication Department, Kolkata
Email: *mail@advaitaashrama.org*
Website: *www.advaitaashrama.org*

© *All Rights Reserved*
First Edition, August 1970
Ninteenth Reprint, January 2012
18M

Script by
Irene Ray and
Mallika Clare Gupta

Illustrated by
Ramananda Banerjee

ISBN 978-81-85301-65-5

Price: ₹ 32

Printed in India at
The Indian Press Private Limited
Kolkata 700 013

Publisher's Note

Joyfully we place this book, *The Story of Vivekananda*, before the children of the world. We hope they will cherish it.

When an absent brother comes home for a while, his brothers and sisters are happy; and when he goes away again, they are sad. Through the pages of this book one who is a big brother to all of us—Vivekananda—comes home, never to go away. He stays on in every home as the guiding light. With him as companion we grow in strength, goodness, and wisdom in a spontaneous way. What is more, he is such fun!

The idea of the book grew from Swami Vishwashrayananda's *Vivekananda for Children*, published by the Swami Vivekananda Birth Centenary Committee, Calcutta, in 1963.

The text of the book has been prepared by Mallika Clare Gupta and Irene R. Ray, two western ladies who have made India their home. To them, and to the artist Ramananda Banerjee, who did the excellent illustrations and designed the cover, we offer our hearty thanks.

May this book bring abiding joy to all who read it!

Advaita Ashrama
Mayavati, 1 August 1970

The Seven Sages

There are seven stars in the sky, which people say are really seven great sages. These sages are always in deep prayer. They are meditating on God.

Once a small boy went there. He was a lovely boy. But there was no one there to see how lovely he was, for all the seven sages had their eyes closed.

The little boy ran up to one of the sages, as if he knew him. He lovingly threw his little arms around the sage's neck. He called

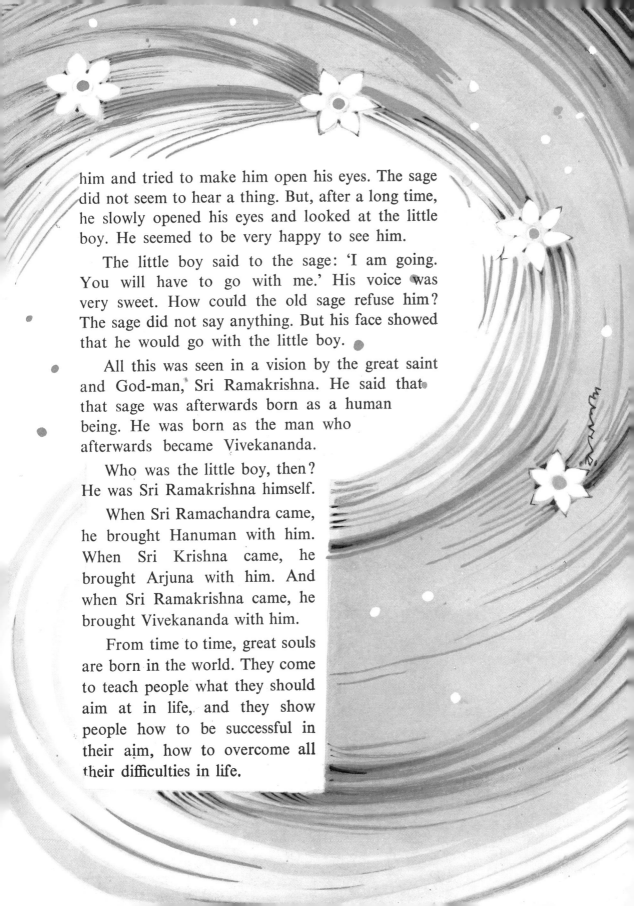

him and tried to make him open his eyes. The sage did not seem to hear a thing. But, after a long time, he slowly opened his eyes and looked at the little boy. He seemed to be very happy to see him.

The little boy said to the sage: 'I am going. You will have to go with me.' His voice was very sweet. How could the old sage refuse him? The sage did not say anything. But his face showed that he would go with the little boy.

All this was seen in a vision by the great saint and God-man, Sri Ramakrishna. He said that that sage was afterwards born as a human being. He was born as the man who afterwards became Vivekananda.

Who was the little boy, then? He was Sri Ramakrishna himself.

When Sri Ramachandra came, he brought Hanuman with him. When Sri Krishna came, he brought Arjuna with him. And when Sri Ramakrishna came, he brought Vivekananda with him.

From time to time, great souls are born in the world. They come to teach people what they should aim at in life, and they show people how to be successful in their aim, how to overcome all their difficulties in life.

A Gift from Shiva

Calcutta is a big city, and part of it is called Simla. In that part of Calcutta, a lady named Bhuvaneshwari used to worship Shiva every day. She would pray to him: 'Lord Shiva, please give me a boy to hold on my lap!' Bhuvaneshwari had several daughters, but she longed for a son. Every day she prayed to Shiva for a son. One of her relatives lived in Varanasi. She asked her to go and worship Vireshwara Shiva for her, at Varanasi.

Bhuvaneshwari prayed and prayed with great faith and devotion. She longed and longed for a son, and at last a son was born to her.

It was the time of the festival marking the end of winter. That year—it was 1863—the festival fell on the 12th January. On this day, every year, people go to bathe in the Ganga. That day, as some women passed the house of Bhuvaneshwari, they heard the loud sound of conch shells being blown. They at once went in to see what their friend was celebrating.

And what did they see? They saw a new-born babe, Bhuvaneshwari's son! He was a big,

chubby baby, with a sweet smile on his face. He had big eyes; they had never seen a baby with such large and wonderful eyes. They thought that he must be a very special baby!

This baby's father was named Vishwanath Datta. He was a lawyer, and he earned much money. He also spent it; he had fine clothes, many servants, and a carriage with a horse. He was also a very good-hearted and generous man. He used to give his money away to people who asked him for it, and who needed it.

Bhuvaneshwari and Vishwanath Datta were very happy with their baby son, born on the 12th January 1863.

Bhuvaneshwari believed that her little son was a gift from Vireshwara Shiva, so she named him Vireshwar (Bireshwar). But that is a big name for such a little baby, isn't it? Everyone began to call him 'Biley', for short.

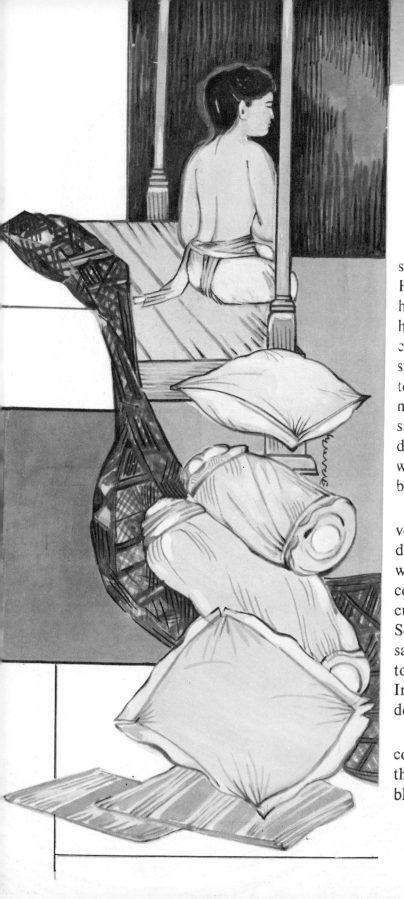

Biley the Naughty Boy

In his childhood, Biley was sometimes a very naughty child. His mother and sisters scolded him many times. Once one of his sisters chased him, but she could not catch him. He ran and stood in a gutter, and called out to her, 'Come here and catch me, if you want!' He knew his sister would not step into that dirty drain, for if she did she would have to go and take a bath.

Sometimes Biley would get very angry. Then no one could do anything with him. He would break everything he could get his hands on, plates, cups, saucers — everything! Sometimes his mother would say: 'I prayed to Lord Shiva to grant me a son like him. Instead, he sent me one of his demons!'

One day there was a great commotion in the house. Biley threw all the pillows and blankets from the bed. His mother scolded him loudly and told him to put them back. But Biley would not do so. He sat facing the wall, and would not speak to anyone.

A pious old lady who lived next door heard all the noise. She asked what was the matter. Bhuvaneshwari said: 'Whenever we ask Biley to do anything against his will, he acts like this. No one can tell him what to do. Biley has a very strong will.'

The old lady replied: 'Bhuvaneshwari dear, Biley has come from Shiva. He is Shiva himself. That is why you cannot force him to do anything.'

When Biley became very, very naughty, there was only one thing his mother could do. She would pour a few pots of water on his head, saying all the while, 'Shiva, Shiva, Shiva!' Biley would then become quiet.

Sometimes she would say to him: 'Biley, if you go on like this, Shiva will not let you go to Kailasa!' Whenever Biley heard this, he would become calm and quiet.

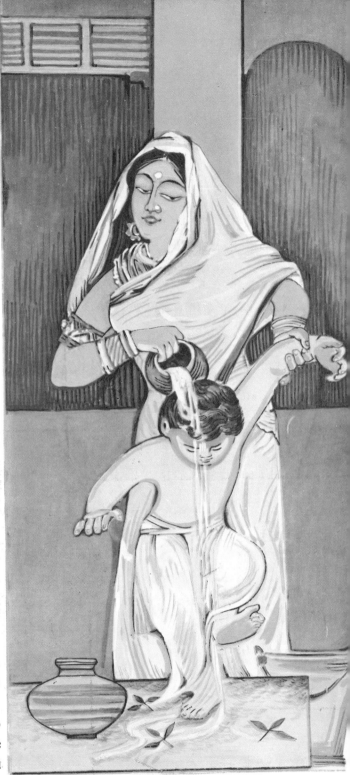

Biley's Loving Heart

Some people are born with kind and loving hearts. They always try to help other people. Biley was like that.

Many sadhus and sannyasins, and beggars too, came to the house almost every day for food or money. Biley used to open the door and give them anything that was handy. He never thought how much it might cost his father! He would give away even the most costly things.

Bhuvaneshwari said: 'How can I run the household with Biley giving away so many things?'

One day, she locked him up in a room upstairs. She said: 'Now, he cannot go to the door and give things away.' She also

thought that it would teach him a good lesson to be locked up!

Biley felt very sad, sitting all alone in the room upstairs. Soon, he heard a beggar calling out. Biley wanted to give the poor man something. He looked around the room. He found one trunk that was not locked. Quickly, Biley opened it and took out some saris.

He opened a window. The beggar was standing just below the window. He was dressed in rags. His body was nothing but bones. Biley felt very sorry for him. Happily, he threw down the saris to the man. The poor beggar was very pleased at this kindness of the little boy.

Biley's Games

All children love to play. Biley, also, used to play many kinds of games. He liked to play marbles and ball games. He also liked to climb trees, as all boys do. Sometimes Biley and his friends would play 'King and Court'. Biley was always the king. Sometimes they would play at being sages. They would sit cross-legged with their hands in their laps, and their eyes tightly closed. They had seen grown-up men and women sit like that, when they were thinking of God.

Biley used to look like a little Buddha when he sat like that. When he played this game, he sat very still with his eyes closed. He would think only of God. He would forget everything else. He did not know what was going on around him. But his friends could not sit still so long. They would close their eyes for a while, and open them now and then to see what the others were doing and what was happening all around them.

One day, when they were playing this game of meditation on the terrace of Biley's house, the boys saw a snake crawling along the floor towards them. It was a deadly cobra!

They jumped up and ran away as fast as they could, shouting: 'Biley! Biley! Come away! Hurry, hurry! There is a big cobra. It will bite you. Run! Run!'

But Biley did not hear them at all. He still sat there with his eyes closed. He was thinking only of God. He did not know what was going on around him.

And what did the cobra do? It moved around on the floor for a while, and then it went away. It did not do any harm to Biley!

Learning Lessons

Biley was a very bright boy. Before he was six years old he knew by heart the stories of the *Ramayana* and the *Mahabharata*. He even knew a whole grammar book by heart! How could such a little boy learn all these things? One of Biley's aunties used to hold him on her lap and read these books to him. Biley could remember everything. He never forgot what he heard, even if he heard it only once.

Biley was now seven years old. He was going to the Metropolitan School. Even before Biley started going to school, he had a tutor. The tutor came to his house every day to teach him. Biley used to sit and listen carefully, while the tutor read the books to him. He always remembered what the tutor read.

How was it possible for Biley to remember everything he heard? It was because he never thought of anything else while the tutor was reading.

So Biley had plenty of time to play. He learned lathi-play, physical exercises, boxing, and many other things. His father bought him a little pony, and he loved to ride it. He was a very happy little boy, and he made all his friends happy, too.

❋

Biley Always Told the Truth

Once the teacher in the geography class asked Biley a question. He answered it. But the teacher said that the answer was wrong. Biley said that the answer was right. The teacher became very angry. He scolded him and gave him a slap! Biley went home and told his mother. He felt very sad about it. His mother said: 'Well, Biley, do not mind what the teacher did.

You must always tell the truth. As long as you know you are right, you need not worry about anything.'

Later, the teacher went to their home. He found that the answer Biley gave was quite correct! So he went to say he was sorry. He told Biley: 'My boy, I am very sorry for what I said and did. I was wrong.'

Another time, Biley was talking during a lesson. The teacher asked him to answer some questions. The teacher thought that he would not know the answers. Then he would punish him for talking. But Biley stood up and answered all the questions, one after the other.

The teacher said: 'Oh, I see, I was mistaken. You were not the boy who was talking. Otherwise, you could not have answered my questions. It must have been some other boy.'

The teacher looked sternly around the class, trying to find out which boy it was.

But Biley said: 'Sir, that is not correct. I answered your questions all right. But I was the boy who was talking!'

All his life, Biley always told the truth.

Don't Accept without Testing

Biley always wanted to test the truth of what he was told. He could not believe anything just because someone said it was true.

Biley and his friends often used to play on a big tree in a neighbour's garden. Biley would climb high up in the tree. Sometimes he would hang from one of the branches and swing back

and forth, holding on with his knees. The boys would shout to each other. They made a lot of noise.

The old grandfather of the house did not like so much noise. One day he went out and shook his fist at Biley.

'Don't climb that tree any more!' he said. 'Don't you know that it is haunted? There is a ghost in that tree, and it will grab you by the neck and kill you!'

Biley quietly listened to the old man and said nothing in reply. But as soon as the man went back into the house, Biley again began to climb the tree.

One of the boys said: 'Oh, Biley, don't climb the tree any more. That ghost will catch you by the neck. That is what the old man said. Please come down, Biley. Let us go home.'

Biley laughed. He said: 'Don't be a donkey! How many times have I climbed this tree! You know that. If a ghost lived in it, he would have caught me long ago.'

When Biley grew up he always told people: 'Have no fear! Ask questions and find out the truth for yourself. Never believe anything, unless you know it is true. Be strong and fearless!'

A Test of Courage

In times of danger, Biley always kept a cool head and did his duty.

There was a sports' club near Biley's house, where the boys used to go for physical

exercises. Once they started to set up a swing. The main pole was very heavy. The boys tried to lift it, but they could not. It was too heavy for them.

There were some people standing on the roadside watching the boys. Among them was an English sailor. When he saw that the boys could not lift the heavy pole, he wanted to help them.

'Boys,' he said, 'I'll help you lift that pole.'

He was a big strong man. Along with the boys, he started to lift the pole. Suddenly, the pole slipped out of their hands. As it fell, it hit the sailor on the head. He fell down with a big cut on his forehead. It was bleeding badly. The sailor lay on the ground very still. The boys thought he was dead. They were very frightened, and most of them ran away.

But Biley and three of his friends did not run away. Biley tore a piece of cloth from his dhoti and quickly bandaged the sailor's head with it. He poured some water on his face and began to fan him.

After a while, the sailor opened his eyes. He was not dead at all! The boys carried him to a schoolhouse which was near by. A doctor came and treated him. Biley and his friends nursed the sailor until he was well. They were glad that they had had the courage to stand by the man who had tried to help them.

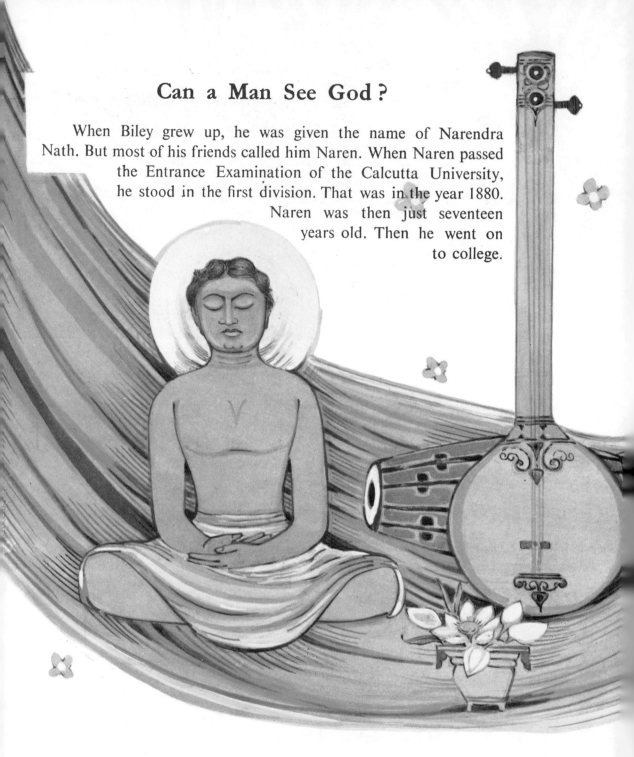

Can a Man See God ?

When Biley grew up, he was given the name of Narendra Nath. But most of his friends called him Naren. When Naren passed the Entrance Examination of the Calcutta University, he stood in the first division. That was in the year 1880. Naren was then just seventeen years old. Then he went on to college.

From his boyhood, Naren had had great faith in God. But now he began to think more about Him. He asked questions and had many doubts.

'Who is God? Where is God? Can we see God?' he asked.

He often sat and thought about these questions. When Naren was a child, he used to play at meditation. Now he began to meditate like a real sage, like a rishi.

Very often he would stay alone in his room for hours. His mother thought that he must be reading his books, but he was not. He was thinking of God. He sometimes sang songs which told about God, and about how people longed to see God. Naren had a beautiful voice, and he knew many songs.

But it is not so easy to think of God. How is it that Naren could think of Him so easily? Naren had always told the truth.

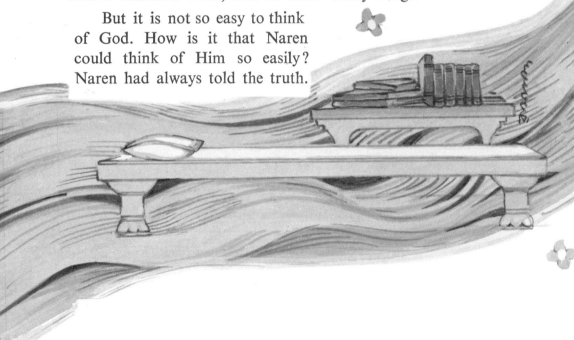

He was as pure as a flower. That is why he could easily think of God. The more Naren thought about God, the more eager he was to see Him. Every day, he became more and more eager to see God.

He wondered if there was any man who had really seen God!

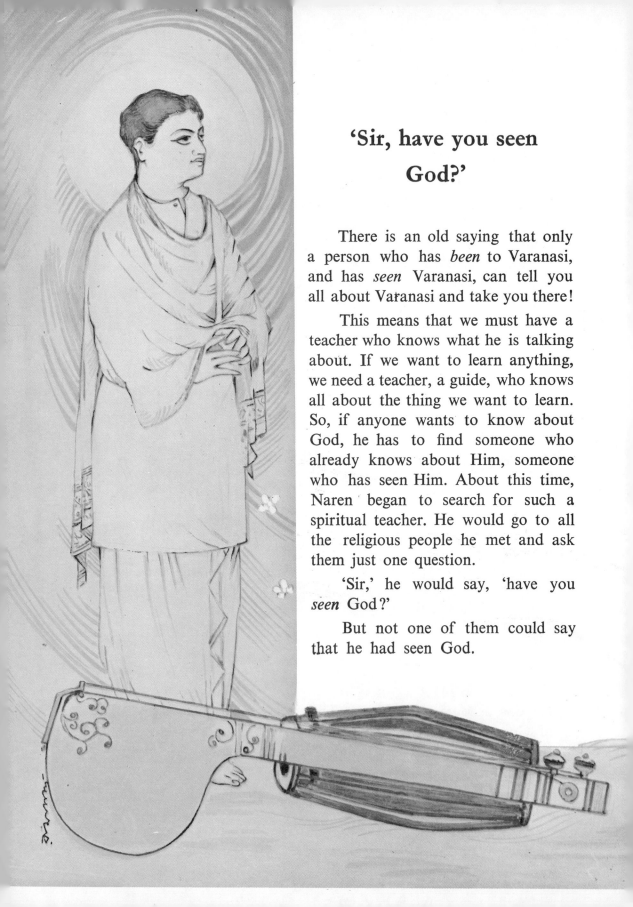

'Sir, have you seen God?'

There is an old saying that only a person who has *been* to Varanasi, and has *seen* Varanasi, can tell you all about Varanasi and take you there!

This means that we must have a teacher who knows what he is talking about. If we want to learn anything, we need a teacher, a guide, who knows all about the thing we want to learn. So, if anyone wants to know about God, he has to find someone who already knows about Him, someone who has seen Him. About this time, Naren began to search for such a spiritual teacher. He would go to all the religious people he met and ask them just one question.

'Sir,' he would say, 'have you *seen* God?'

But not one of them could say that he had seen God.

One day, one of Naren's neighbours asked him to go and sing at his house. He had as his honoured guest the great teacher, *Sri Ramakrishna*. This neighbour wanted Naren to sing for Sri Ramakrishna, because Naren sang so beautifully.

Sri Ramakrishna was very pleased with the songs Naren sang. He liked Naren, too; and he asked him to go to the Dakshineswar temple, where he lived, and sing for him there.

That was the very first meeting between Sri Ramakrishna and Narendra Nath.

After that meeting, Narendra wondered if Sri Ramakrishna was a real teacher. People said that Sri Ramakrishna had seen God.

Narendra decided that he would go to Sri Ramakrishna and ask him if he had seen God.

Sri Ramakrishna
Gives the Answer

One day, Naren went to Dakshineswar to see Sri Ramakrishna. Sri Ramakrishna was very happy to see him. He brought some sweets and fed Naren as if he were a small child. He was like a loving mother to him.

Suddenly, Naren asked the question he had asked so many other religious men, the question he had come to ask.

'Sir,' he said, 'have you seen God?'

Sri Ramakrishna replied: 'Oh, yes, indeed, I have!'

Naren looked at Sri Ramakrishna in astonishment.

'I see him as clearly as I see you,' added Sri Ramakrishna. 'One can see and talk with Him as I do with you.'

Naren was surprised at this answer; and he was delighted. He listened carefully to all that Sri Ramakrishna said.

'This is the spiritual teacher I have been searching for!' he thought to himself. So Naren became his disciple.

Naren knew that Sri Ramakrishna was a man who had seen God. Still, he would not accept anything he said without asking questions about it. This pleased Sri Ramakrishna. He wanted the boys who came to him to think for themselves and to ask questions.

Sri Ramakrishna had said that he could not stand the touch of money, or metal. Naren wondered about this. One day, when no one was in the room, he put a silver rupee under the mattress of Sri Ramakrishna's bed. Sri Ramakrishna came and sat on the bed. He jumped up, as if stung by a scorpion!

'What has happened to my bed?' he asked.

The bed was searched, and the rupee was found. All this while, Naren was standing in a corner, and saying nothing. Sri Ramakrishna knew that Naren had done it, and he was pleased.

Naren's Prayer

Sri Ramakrishna loved Naren very much, and Naren also loved him with all his heart. It is only when there is a great and pure love between a Guru and his disciple that the disciple can be taught about God. The Guru awakens God in the disciple.

Naren became a disciple of Sri Ramakrishna, and he was very, very happy. He used to go to Dakshineswar very often, and hear about God. About this time, a very sad thing happened. Naren's father died. The family was now very poor. Sometimes they did not even have enough to eat. Naren felt very sad. He decided to try to get a job.

Naren was a brilliant student. He had his B.A. degree. Still he could not find any work. He walked from one office to another, but he could not get work. He thought: 'What will become of my mother, sisters, and brothers if I cannot earn some money?'

One day, he told everything to Sri Ramakrishna.

'Naren, today is Tuesday,' Sri Ramakrishna replied, 'whatever you ask of Mother today She will give you. You ask Her.'

That evening, Naren went to the temple of Kali to pray. When he came back, Sri Ramakrishna asked him, 'What did Mother say?'

'Oh, I forgot to ask Her!' cried Naren.

'You forgot? Go back at once. Hurry!' said Sri Ramakrishna.

This time also the same thing happened!

The third time Naren returned, looking very peaceful. He told Sri Ramakrishna: 'How could I ask Mother for money? It would be like asking a great king for a pumpkin! I could only ask Her for devotion, for selfless love, and for the power to understand Her!'

Afterwards, Sri Ramakrishna told Naren that his family would never lack the bare necessities of life. Only then did Naren feel that it was right for him not to try to earn money.

That night, Sri Ramakrishna taught Naren a beautiful song about the Mother. Naren sang that song the whole night through, while Sri Ramakrishna sat in deep meditation.

The Baranagore Monastery

After some time, Sri Ramakrishna became ill. He was taken to a garden-house in Cossipore, near Calcutta. Naren and the other boys went there to stay with him and nurse him. When they were not busy nursing Sri Ramakrishna, they spent their time meditating.

One night Naren went into very deep meditation. He had a spiritual experience which filled him with bliss. He told Sri Ramakrishna that he wanted to stay in meditation all the time.

'No, Naren,' Sri Ramakrishna said, 'there is much work for you to do. First, do your work. Then you may stay in meditation.'

Sri Ramakrishna did not get any better. He became more and more ill. He could not live much longer.

One day, he said to Naren: 'I have given you all my spiritual power. With this great power, you will help all the people in the world. You will teach them how to love God and how to know God. You will help the poor, too.'

Naren was still a young boy. He did not understand how these words of his Guru could be true. How could he teach people these things? How could he help the poor?

It was on the 16th August 1886 that Sri Ramakrishna left his body. The boys felt very sad, for they missed him so much! He was like both father and mother to them.

Then they said: 'Yes, Sri Ramakrishna has left his body. But he is still with us. He lives in our hearts.'

After that the boys left their homes and became sannyasins. Their first monastery was a tumble-down house, so old that hissing cobras lived under it. Sometimes the boys had nothing to eat. But they did not mind. They talked and thought of nothing but God.

It was while he was at the Baranagore Math that Naren began to think of what Sri Ramakrishna had said. How was he going to teach people and help them to overcome the sufferings of life? That was the question in Naren's mind.

Swami Vivekananda's Travels in India

A sannyasin always takes a new name. Naren's new name was *Swami Vivekananda*. A respectful way of referring to him is *Swamiji*. So now we shall begin to call him Swamiji.

Swamiji made up his mind to go on a long journey. He wanted to see how the people lived. India is a big country. It is the home of many different kinds of people. Swamiji wanted to see them all.

So he set out on foot, taking with him only a change of clothing, a kamandalu or waterpot, a few books, and a big staff. He walked through villages and towns. He slept under trees. He ate whatever was given to him. Sometimes he stayed in the huts of sweepers, and sometimes he was the guest of kings.

Once, at Varanasi, as Swamiji was coming out of the temple of Mother Durga, he was surrounded by a large number of chattering monkeys. They seemed to be threatening him. Swamiji did not want them to catch hold of him, so he started to run away. But the monkeys chased him.

An old sannyasin was there, watching those monkeys. He called out to Swamiji, 'Stop! Face the brutes!'

Swamiji stopped. He turned round and faced the monkeys. At once, they ran away.

Many years later, Swamiji said: 'If you ever feel afraid of anything, always turn round and *face* it. Never think of running away.'

Swamiji travelled through forests and jungles and then went up to the snow-covered Himalayas. He visited the beautiful temples and sacred places of pilgrimage. Then he went to the west of India and walked through the hot deserts there.

Then Swamiji went to Bombay. From Bombay he went to Bangalore, then to Cochin and Madurai, and then to Rameswaram. Wherever he went, he saw the misery of the poor people.

'I Hit upon a Plan'

At the time when Swami Vivekananda was going from place to place in India, the condition of the country was very bad. India was not a free country then. It was ruled by the British. The people had become very poor. Most people did not have enough to eat.

Very few boys and girls could go to school. People had lost their courage. They had no faith in themselves. They were crushed and helpless. When Swamiji saw this, he wept. He thought of how great India had been in the past. He thought of the great saints and sages. He wept to see how low that great nation had fallen. For many nights he could not sleep. He was thinking and thinking how his country could become great again

When he finally reached the end of his wanderings, he was at Cape Comorin, the farthest end of India in the south. There, at Kanya-Kumari, is a temple of the Divine Mother in the form of a little girl. Every day the priests of the temple decorate the image with sandal paste. The little Mother has lovely eyes and a beautiful smile. She looks very wonderful!

This temple stands just near the seashore. As you look out over the ocean, you see some big rocks standing up out of the water. The waves are constantly dashing against the rocks. Beyond them, for miles and miles and miles, there is nothing but endless water!

One day, Swamiji swam through those dashing waves to the rocks. He climbed up and sat on the very last one of them. From there, looking at his beloved Motherland, he wept again to think of the misery of all her children. Swamiji had two great loves—his Guru, Sri Ramakrishna, and Mother India! While he was sitting on that rock, Swamiji went into deep meditation. It was then that he found out what should be done to make India great again.

'Sitting on that last bit of Indian rock,' he said, 'I hit upon a plan. I hit upon a plan.'

Journey to the West

Swamiji swam back to the shore. He then went to Madras. There he had many disciples. He told them that in his travels he had found that India was asleep. India was like a person who had been asleep for hundreds of years. She had to be awakened.

Swamiji now explained the plan he had thought of. He would go away from India. He would see what the people in other countries were doing. They had faith in themselves, so they could do anything. Also he would tell them all about India.

India believes that nothing is stronger than the spirit that is in man. But now India has forgotten this. She has no faith.

'Our people have lost faith in themselves,' said Swamiji sadly: 'I will bring back that faith to them. Now I go; but when I return, I shall awaken the sleeping millions of my people.'

A Parliament of Religions was to be held in America, in the city of Chicago. Leaders of all the different religions of the world were going to speak.

'I will go there,' Swamiji said, 'I will tell them about the ancient religion of India. I will tell them what I know, and I will learn from them the things they know.'

Chicago was many thousands of miles away. To get there, money was needed. Swamiji's disciples in Madras collected money. And the Raja of Khetri, one of his disciples, also gave him much help. But Swamiji said that he was not yet ready to go. He said: 'I shall not go, until I know that God wants me to go. If it is God's plan, I shall go, otherwise not.'

One day, Swamiji was standing on the seashore looking at the beautiful sea and thinking about his plan. Then he saw a marvellous thing. In a vision, he saw Sri Ramakrishna walking on the sea. He was asking Swamiji, by signs, to follow him! Now Swamiji knew that it was his duty to go to America. It was the wish of Sri Ramakrishna.

It was on the 31st May 1893 that Swami Vivekananda sailed for America. He boarded the ship at Bombay. The Captain gave his orders. The ship's whistle sounded a long, loud blast; and the ship sailed out of the harbour.

Swamiji watched the shores of India until they faded into the distance. Mother India **faded** from his sight. But she stayed in his heart and he never **ceased** to serve her.

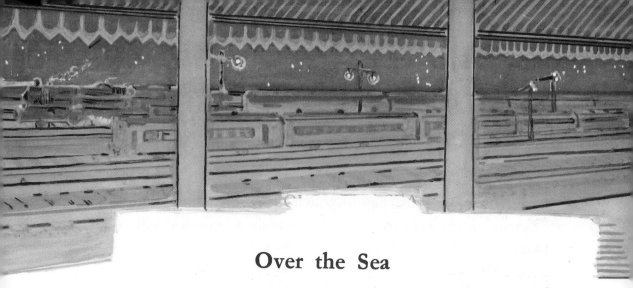

Over the Sea

The ship that carried Swamiji to America stopped at several places on the way. It went to Singapore, Hong Kong, China, and to several ports in Japan. Swamiji was eager to see all those places and the different people in each country. From Japan the ship crossed the wide Pacific Ocean. Then it reached Vancouver, in Canada. At that place Swamiji left the ship and went by train to Chicago, in America.

A big exhibition was being held in Chicago. The Parliament of Religions was a part of that. But it was to start some weeks later. Swamiji went to tell the organizers that he would speak at the Parliament.

What a surprise and disappointment! He was told that it was too late.

'Everything has been settled,' said the man in charge. 'It is too late now. No more people will be allowed to speak.' Swamiji did not know what to do. Should he go back to India? But what about his plan, for which he had come so many thousands of miles?

It was two months before the Parliament would begin. It cost a lot of money to live in Chicago. Swamiji did not have so much money with him. Someone told him to go to another city, Boston. There it would not cost so much. So he went to Boston and stayed there for a while. Then he went back to Chicago.

The evening he arrived in Chicago Swamiji had nowhere to stay. In India, he would have slept on the railway platform. But in America that was not allowed. Swamiji saw some empty packing

cases near the railway station. He climbed into one of them and spent the night there. Swamiji had had nothing to eat that day. He was feeling very hungry. But he did not feel sorry for himself. He was always thinking of the poor people of his country. How much more they were suffering, he thought.

On the Streets of Chicago

The next morning, Swamiji crawled out of the packing case! He was feeling stiff from sitting in that box all night. And now he was more hungry than ever. But he had work to do.

In Boston Swamiji had met a famous man. His name was Professor John Henry Wright, of Harvard University. Professor Wright liked Swamiji very much. He was surprised to find how much Swamiji had learned. He wrote to one of his friends: 'Swami Vivekananda is more learned than all our learned professors put together.'

Professor Wright had given Swamiji a letter to a friend in

Chicago. This person would see that Swamiji would be allowed to speak at the Parliament. But Swamiji had lost the address of the office where he was to go. Chicago was a very big city. Swamiji went from street to street trying to find the office But he could not find it.

By this time, Swamiji was very tired and in great need of food. He went to a few houses and begged for food, just as he would have done in India. But America was not India! No one gave him anything. They drove him away. Some people even insulted him!

Swamiji could walk no more. He sat down on the pavement. He could not think what to do. Just then, the door of a house on the other side of the street opened. A lady came over to Swamiji and asked him if he had come to Chicago for the Parliament of Religions. She then invited him into her home and treated him as an honoured guest. She asked him to stay in her house. Her name was Mrs. Hale. She and her husband, George Hale, became Swamiji's great friends. He stayed in their home whenever he went to Chicago.

That very day, Mrs. Hale took Swamiji in her carriage to the office of the Parliament of Religions. It was agreed that Swamiji would speak at the Parliament on the Hindu religion.

At the Parliament of Religions

The Parliament of Religions began on the 11th September 1893. It was held in a large hall, called the Hall of Columbus.

On the platform sat the speakers. There were more than sixty of them, and they had come from all the different countries in the world. Swamiji sat in the front row. About seven thousand American men and women sat in the hall. They had come to hear these famous men speak about their religions.

One after the other, they spoke. Swamiji felt a little frightened. Never before in his life had he spoken before such a big crowd of people. At last, he got up and walked to the front of the platform.

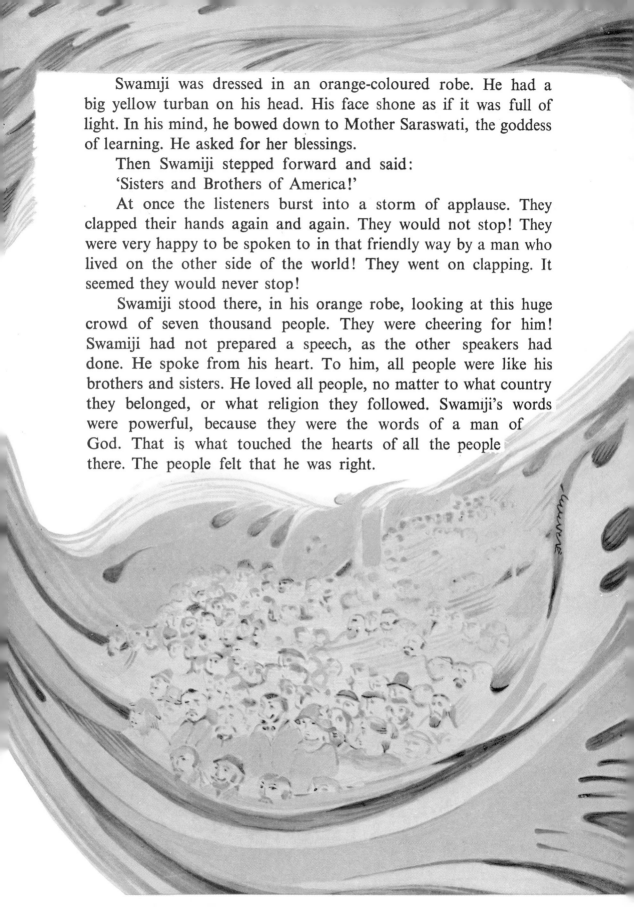

Swamiji was dressed in an orange-coloured robe. He had a big yellow turban on his head. His face shone as if it was full of light. In his mind, he bowed down to Mother Saraswati, the goddess of learning. He asked for her blessings.

Then Swamiji stepped forward and said:

'Sisters and Brothers of America!'

At once the listeners burst into a storm of applause. They clapped their hands again and again. They would not stop! They were very happy to be spoken to in that friendly way by a man who lived on the other side of the world! They went on clapping. It seemed they would never stop!

Swamiji stood there, in his orange robe, looking at this huge crowd of seven thousand people. They were cheering for him! Swamiji had not prepared a speech, as the other speakers had done. He spoke from his heart. To him, all people were like his brothers and sisters. He loved all people, no matter to what country they belonged, or what religion they followed. Swamiji's words were powerful, because they were the words of a man of God. That is what touched the hearts of all the people there. The people felt that he was right.

Vivekananda in America

After the people had stopped their cheering and clapping, Swamiji began his speech. The speech he made that day made him famous throughout the world.

He said that he was proud to belong to a religion which had taught people to accept all religions as true. His country, India, had given shelter to many people when they were not allowed to follow their own religions in their own countries.

He then told them about a hymn which was repeated every day by millions of people in India. The hymn said that just as different rivers all meet in the sea, so the different religions all meet in the one Lord of the universe.

The next day, big pictures of Swamiji were put up in the streets of Chicago. People wrote about him in the newspapers.

After the Parliament was over Swamiji travelled all over America. Wherever he went, he gave lectures and talked to the people. He answered their questions and told them about India.

In those days, people in western countries did not know much about India, and they had many wrong ideas about her. It was through Swamiji that they came to know and respect India.

People said: 'Swami Vivekananda is not only a great spiritual teacher. He is also a great patriot. When he says the words "my country", we feel how much he loves India!'

It was not only the grown-ups in America who loved Swamiji,

children loved him too. Once Swamiji was watching some boys. They were standing on a bridge trying to shoot at egg-shells that were floating on the river. The egg-shells bobbed up and down. The boys could not hit any of them. They fired the gun many times, but they always missed the target!

They noticed that Swamiji was watching them. So they called out to him: 'Well, you are watching us. Do you think you can do better?'

Swamiji smiled and said: 'I will try.'

Then the boys said: 'It's not so easy as you think!'

Swamiji took the gun and aimed at the egg-shells. He stood very still for a few minutes. Then he fired the gun. He fired twelve times, and every time he hit an egg-shell! The boys were very surprised. How could any man shoot egg-shells like that? they thought. They said to Swamiji: 'Well, Mister, how did you do it?'

Swamiji laughed. He liked the boys.

'Whatever you are doing,' he said, 'put your whole mind on it. If you are shooting, your mind should be only on the target. Then you will never miss. If you are learning your lessons, think only of the lesson. In my country boys are taught to do this.'

In England

From America, Swamiji went to England. He crossed the Atlantic Ocean in a big ship. In England, also, he taught many people. The newspapers in London said that Swamiji was a great soul, like the Buddha and Christ. People listened to him very carefully, and went regularly to his classes. In both America and England Swamiji made many friends and disciples. Only one of these is well known to us in India. Her name was Miss Margaret Noble. But Swamiji called her 'Nivedita', which means 'one who is dedicated'.

Sister Nivedita was a very

learned lady with great courage. Just like the great women of India, Sister Nivedita wanted to know about God. She became a nun in order to follow all Swamiji's teachings. Sister Nivedita looked upon India as her

own country. She came to India and started a school for girls. She dedicated herself to India and served the people of India for the rest of her life.

Many more people from western countries became friends of India. Some of them came to India, on a pilgrimage, to see the country where Sri Ramakrishna and Swami Vivekananda were born.

Swamiji used to say: 'When you know the English people, and when they know you, they are your very good friends.' We have to know people to understand them. 'The Englishman is bold, brave, and steady', he said. 'The American people are very warm-hearted, and they make a guest feel welcome at once,' Swamiji went on. 'In that country, the feeling of brotherhood is very strong. If you meet a man only for five minutes, he will invite you to his home and treat you like a brother.'

When Swamiji was leaving England to return to India, many people were very sad. They had tears in their eyes. One man said that it was a grey and gloomy day outside; and in the hearts of Swamiji's friends, it was also grey and gloomy. Swamiji was dressed in his orange robe, and his face was bright. He looked like a bright ray of sunshine on that dark day in London.

Swamiji said 'good-bye' to the West. He had given his message to the West, and it had been received by hundreds of people. They loved and respected Swamiji.

Return to the Motherland

After travelling in America, England, and the Continent, Swamiji began the journey back to India.

A friend asked him: 'Swamiji, you have lived so long in the wealthy countries of the west. How will you feel now about your own poor country?'

To this Swamiji replied: 'India I loved before I came away. Now the very dust of India has become holy to me, the very air is now to me holy, it is now the holy land, the place of pilgrimage.'

Later, when Swamiji was speaking to the people of Ramnad, a place in the south of India, he said much more about his motherland. It was now clear to him that India had a message to give to the world: that all people are one in spirit. The world is one big family.

'This is the motherland of philosophy, of spirituality, and of ethics, of sweetness, gentleness, and love. These still exist, and

my experience of the world leads me to stand on firm ground and make the bold statement that India is still the first and foremost of all the nations of the world in these respects. ... Great works are to be done, wonderful powers have to be worked out, we have to teach other nations many things.'

Swamiji reached Colombo, in Ceylon, on the 15th January 1897. Thousands of people were waiting to greet him. Big arches were put up in the main streets. Swamiji was garlanded by many people. He walked in a procession to a pandal, where he was to speak. People threw flower petals in his path. One man held a large umbrella over him. He was treated like a great king. People shouted: 'Jai Mahadeva!' Victory to the great God Shiva! Some people sang songs that were more than two thousand years old.

From Colombo, he came to Jaffna. Then he crossed the sea and landed at Pamban. He was received there by the Raja of Ramnad. Then he passed through many other towns in South India. Wherever he went, thousands of people welcomed him with the highest honour. And the cities were beautifully decorated for his home-coming. Swamiji gave stirring speeches wherever he went. People were wild with excitement. Today, when we read those speeches, we too feel inspired and are filled with enthusiasm for the greatness of India and India's work in the world.

Swamiji said: 'This is India! These receptions are not for a politician, or for a soldier, or a millionaire. They are for a begging sannyasin. Only in India could such things happen. This is the greatness of India, this love for God and for those who seek God.'

Swamiji in Madras

Long before Swamiji reached Madras, the people of that city were planning to welcome him. It was from Madras that Swamiji had left for the West, taking his ship at Bombay. The people of Madras felt that he was *their* Swamiji. And so he was!

Swamiji was coming by train from Kumbakonam. It was a through train, and it did not stop at small stations. But at every station there were large crowds of people waiting to get a glimpse of the great Swamiji! At one small station, near Madras, the people wanted very much to see Swamiji. 'Please,' they begged the Station-master, 'flag Swamiji's train and make it stop. We *must* see Swamiji!' 'I can understand your feelings,' said the Station-master, 'but I cannot stop the train. It is a through train, and it will not stop here.'

What could the people do? They saw the train in the distance. It was coming very fast. About a hundred people ran and lay down on the tracks, in front of the rushing train! The Station-master was frightened. He had to stop the train! Then the people ran to Swamiji's compartment and garlanded him and asked for his blessings. Swamiji stood there, radiant with love for them. He blessed them, and the train moved on.

At last the train reached Madras. Again, there was a huge crowd to greet him. He was garlanded, and many people threw flower petals as he walked.

They cheered and shouted: 'Welcome, Prince of Men', and 'Hail to Sri Ramakrishna's worthy disciple'.

The streets were decorated with arches and flags and flowers. All the shops were closed. The people filled the streets. Swamiji was taken by carriage through the streets of Madras. Some young men took the horses away from Swamiji's carriage and pulled it themselves through the streets. Never before in Madras had there been such a welcome for anyone!

Swamiji was taken to a large hall, and there addresses of welcome were read to him. Wave after wave of people surrounded Swamiji. It became impossible for him to give a long speech. So he said: 'I am intensely pleased at the show of enthusiasm. That is what is required—tremendous enthusiasm. Only make it permanent; keep it up. . . . We want to work out great things in India. For that I require your help; such enthusiasm is necessary.'

A day or two later, Swamiji was able to give a long speech to
the people. He called it 'My Plan of Campaign', and in it he said:
'Make your nerves strong. What we want is muscles of iron and
nerves of steel. ... Stand on your feet and be men.' Today, if
we want to serve India, we should first understand Swamiji's ideas
and then follow them in our lives. If you want to serve India, he

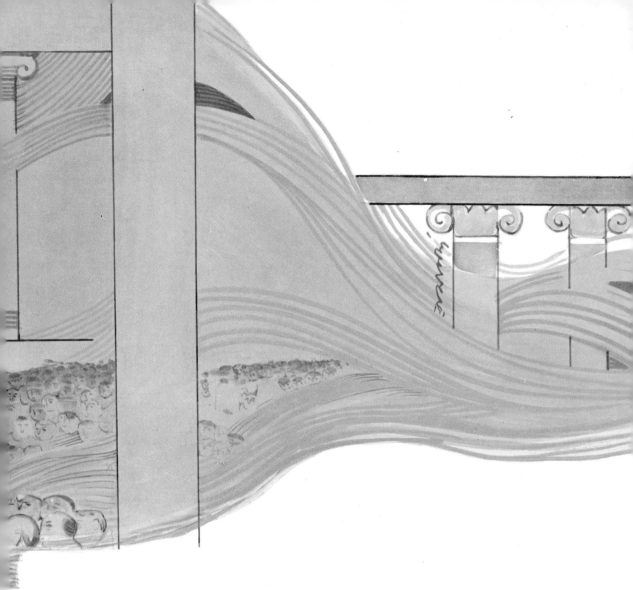

said, three things are necessary. First, you must have great feeling. Love is the gate to all the secrets of the universe. If you want to help the people who are starving and living in ignorance, you must feel for them, you must love them. Secondly, you must find a practical way to help them. Mere talking will not do. Thirdly, you must have a strong will. Even if the whole world stands against you, you must still dare to do what you think is right. If you have these three things you will work wonders. You will be powerful. Even if you live in a cave your thought will go vibrating all over the world and help people. Such is the power of thought, of sincerity, and of purity of purpose.

The Great Hero Returns Home

It was on the 20th February 1897 that Swamiji returned to Calcutta. How proud the people were! So many years before, the little boy Biley had played in the streets of this city. Now, he was returning as the world-famous hero, Swami Vivekananda.

There were thousands and thousands of people waiting to welcome him. The city was decorated with arches. Banners were flying, and conchs were being blown. The crowds shouted: 'Jai Swami Vivekanandaji ki jai! Jai Sri Ramakrishna ki jai!' Victory to Swami Vivekananda! Glory to Sri Ramakrishna!

Just as in Madras, some young men took the horses away from Swamiji's carriage and pulled it through the streets themselves. To be Swamiji's 'horses' was a great honour! The people crowded around his carriage. There was a sea of people all around. People, people, everywhere! Dressed in an orange robe, Swamiji looked like a royal hero, a great warrior returning after a victorious battle.

And, indeed, that is just what he was. He was a warrior who had conquered the world. But he did not have any soldiers or guns.

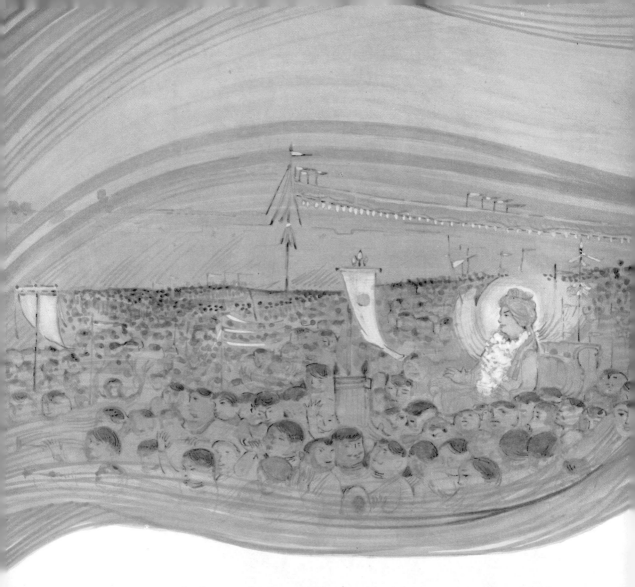

He conquered the world by his great love and by his wonderful message. Swamiji taught people everywhere how they could live in peace and happiness, without fighting.

In Calcutta, day and night, people flocked to see Swamiji. At a big meeting, the city of Calcutta gave Swamiji a public address. At least five thousand people went to that meeting. There were rajas, maharajas, sannyasins, pundits, and all the important people of Calcutta, and a group of European ladies and gentlemen. Hundreds of school boys and college students were also there.

In his reply to the address, Swamiji spoke freely and frankly

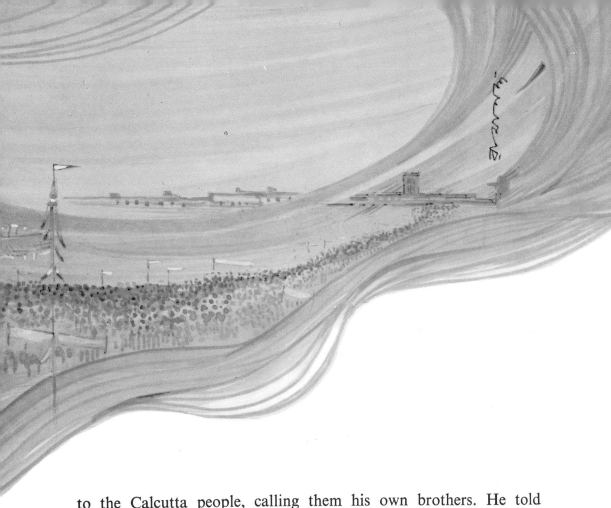

to the Calcutta people, calling them his own brothers. He told them about his work in America and England, and he told them about Sri Ramakrishna. He explained how the great power of Sri Ramakrishna could help India and the world.

He called upon the people of Bengal to be fearless and sacrifice themselves for their country with energy, enthusiasm, and faith. The great work before them was to make known to the whole world the eternal spiritual truths taught by their forefathers. This would raise India once more to her proper spiritual place.

Wherever he went, Swamiji explained his ideas to the people. The speeches he gave are all carefully preserved for us. When we read them today, we feel that he is speaking to us, telling us how we can serve our Motherland.

His call to India, his call to the whole world, was 'Arise, awake, and stop not till the goal is reached.'

Service to God in Man

After his hard work in the West, Swamiji rested for a while at Darjeeling, a hill-station in the Himalayas. Then something happened that made him take up active life again.

There was a dreadful sickness in Calcutta at that time. Many people were dying of it. No one wanted to nurse the sick people, because they were frightened of catching this terrible disease. It was called the plague.

Swamiji called his brother-monks and his disciples together.

'We shall go and nurse these sick people,' he said, 'we shall open a hospital, and we ourselves shall nurse those who have this awful disease.'

'But, Swamiji, where is the money to do such work?' someone asked.

Swamiji was like a man on fire.

'Money?' he thundered. 'Do not bother yourself about money. Get on with this work of service. If I have to, I shall sell the new Math and give all that money for this work!' Swamiji continued: 'Do you not remember that Sri Ramakrishna told us that we should serve God in man? This is service to God in man. It must be done!'

But he did not have to sell the Math. Money came, and the work was done. Finally, the plague was over, and people got well again.

At one time, there were some workmen at the Math who were Santhals. Swamiji loved them very much. One of them was named Kesto.

'Kesto,' said Swamiji, 'how would you like me to give you all a feast?'

They were all very happy. Swamiji gave them a big feast and watched them eat, as if he were their loving mother!

'Today, I have fed God himself,' he said.

Swamiji started centres in other parts of India also. There the monks served the sick and the poor. They helped people in times of famine and flood.

The monks also opened hospitals and schools. They served people of all religions, not only Hindus. Sri Ramakrishna and Swamiji always said that all religions lead to the same God, the Mother of the universe. So we should love all people, because they are our own brothers and sisters.

A New Math at Belur

Many boys and young men began to follow Swamiji. Many of them became sannyasins and worked for the good of the Motherland. They gave up their homes and everything else, so that they could lead good and holy lives and serve India.

Swamiji wanted to have a bigger Math. He got some land just beside the Ganga, near Calcutta, and built a nice Math there. It is called Belur Math, for it is in a village named Belur.

On the 9th December 1898, Swamiji opened the new Math. That day, there was a big celebration. Many people went there from Calcutta and from other parts of India for this grand occasion. Musicians were singing and playing, drummers were beating their drums, and groups of people were singing songs about God. A long procession of monks, headed by Swamiji, went to the shrine to worship. Swamiji prayed to Sri Ramakrishna: 'Lord, please stay

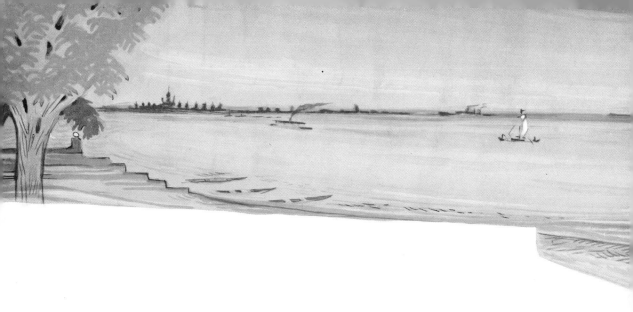

here. Bless us all. Bless all those who come here and all people everywhere in the world.'

Swamiji said that more and more men would join the Math. He also said that some day the women of India would have their own Math. All that came true. Today, there are hundreds of monks of the Order of Sri Ramakrishna, and there is a Math for women called Sarada Math.

'This Math', Swamiji said, 'will harmonize all creeds, all view points. Just as Sri Ramakrishna held highly liberal views, this Math, too, will be a centre for propagating similar ideas. The blazing light of universal harmony that will emanate from here will flood the whole world.'

Living at the Math, Swamiji continued to teach all who went to him. His ideas can be of great help to us today. He said, for example: 'I see it clear as daylight that you all have infinite power in you. Rouse that up; arise, arise! It is better to wear out than to rust out, especially for the sake of doing good to others! On another occasion, Swamiji said, 'We want faith, faith in ourselves. Strength is life; weakness is death.'

Swamiji also said that all should be treated as equal. It is the same spirit that exists in all people. One man should not have plenty of things to enjoy, and another hardly anything. All should have equal rights, based on love for all.

Swamiji's Last Meditation

Swamiji's friends and disciples in America wanted him to go and visit them again. They were longing to see him. So Swamiji went once more to the West and was again intensely active.

This time he was abroad only for about a year and a half. On his way back to India he visited many places in Europe and also in Egypt. But now his health had broken down. He hurried home.

Reaching Belur Math, he said that he wanted to be still and quiet. He felt tired. Swamiji had some pets. He liked to play with them. There was Bagha, a dog; Hamsi, a goat; and Matru, a little baby goat. He also had a tame deer, some ducks, and some cranes. Swamiji would spend many happy hours with these pets.

Swamiji thought more and more of the days when he was a young boy, when he first came to Sri Ramakrishna. Swamiji remembered everything Sri Ramakrishna had told him. How many days had passed since then! Swamiji had gone round the world to do the work of Sri Ramakrishna. The people of India had been fast asleep. Now they were waking up; and Swamiji wanted to rest finally.

Most of the time at the Math, he would pass into deep meditation. He would look like Shiva or the Buddha. What a wonderful scene it was!

On the 4th July 1902, Swamiji sat down to meditate in his room at Belur Math. It was evening. He told the monks he wanted to be alone.

Later when some of them went to see him, they found he had passed away. They saw only his body there.

Swamiji's work was done. He had seen what India needed, and he had told her how to get it. To become great, he said, India must carry forward her own ancient ideal that the greatest strength is spiritual strength. This ideal India must now carry into her everyday life as a modern nation. She must accept all the material benefits of modern science, but she must preserve her spiritual ideals and teach them to the whole world.

His message was given. He could do no more. It was for India now to choose whether she would accept his message or ignore it.

Today, we salute the great Swami and do him honour. And as we do so, we remember that there is no better way to honour a teacher than to try to put into practice all that he taught.

India's Awakening

It was in 1897 that Swamiji told the people: 'For the next fifty years let Mother India be your God. Serve your country as you would serve God, and India will awaken!'

Not long after that, men and women sacrificed their homes, their wealth, and even their lives for their country's freedom.

From 1897 to 1947 is exactly fifty years. Fifty years after Swamiji spoke those words, India achieved independence from British rule. It was the first great step of the awakening Swamiji had described. Without political independence the national awakening could not come, for freedom is essential to growth and development.

Swamiji said that political ideals and political leaders have no real power in India; nor have social ideals or commercial ideals. The only ideal that has real and lasting power in India is the ideal that is based on inner strength. It is a spiritual ideal that says that the soul of man is more powerful than anything else. That is India's national ideal, and when she puts this ideal into practice in her daily life, she will be strong and powerful.

If it is true that the soul of man is more powerful than anything else, then this ideal is true for all people everywhere. So Swamiji said that Indians should now go out into the world and mix with other nations and tell them about this great ideal.

When Indians do that, then will come the awakening of India that Swamiji spoke about. Using the great power that lies in the soul of men, India will spread peacefully throughout the world the equality and justice and sharing of benefits that so many people are now fighting for.

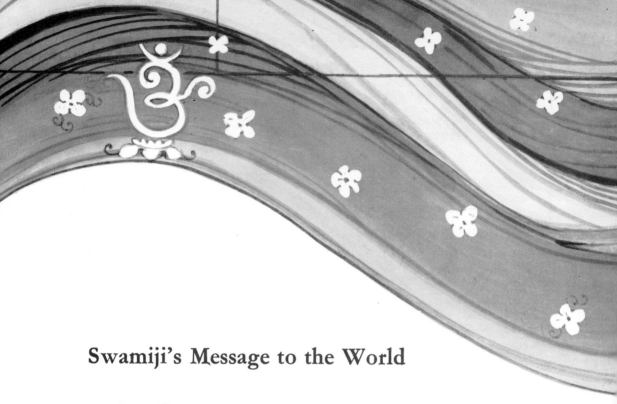

Swamiji's Message to the World

Swamiji very often used the word 'Vedanta', when he was talking about spiritual things. He used this word because he thought it was one which everyone in the whole world could use without giving up his own religious ideas.

The world is full of many different kinds of people, with many different ideas. Swamiji used the word 'Vedanta' to provide a common meeting ground for them all, whatever their ideas might be.

Vedanta, as Swamiji used it, means that from the spiritual standpoint the world is one. There is one Spirit or Ground, and everything that exists in the universe is an expression of that one Spirit. There is nothing other than that one Spirit, nothing separate from it. Everything has its existence within that one Spirit.

This means that if one person seeks God, another seeks Good, another seeks Beauty, another seeks scientific truth, another seeks the perfect society, and another seeks happiness, and so on and on—they are all seeking the same thing, although they express it in different ways. Sri Ramakrishna expressed the same idea very simply. He said that the word for 'water' varied from language to language. Nevertheless, water was the same everywhere in the world.

The idea that everything in the universe exists within one universal Spirit is really a very simple idea, and it is an idea that may be found all over the world, in ancient times and in modern times. In India, this idea was taught very clearly and in great detail in the Upanishads. There it was called 'the science of the Spirit', because people studied it and experimented with it, just as modern people study and experiment with the physical sciences.

Then came Sri Ramakrishna, and he took up this idea and experimented with it in a new way. He himself adopted all the different modes of thought he could find. He took them up, one by one, and practised them to see what they felt like, and to see where they would lead. What he proved by his experiments was that whoever sincerely followed any path would be led ultimately to that one Spirit of the universe, the Ground of all existence. It was true for all people, no matter what religion they followed, or even if they had no religion.

Swamiji, in his turn, took this idea and applied it to the modern world. He said that in particular it must be applied in modern western countries and in modern India. Both, he said, would have to put this idea into practice, but in different ways.

Western people had become more and more interested in science and the application of science to everyday life. But all their study was based on the idea that man was separate from nature, and that men were separate from each other. They were seeking truth, but they were seeking it in physical things. By giving them the idea of Vedanta, Swamiji showed them that they would understand the universe and themselves only when they perceived everything in the light of one basic spiritual unity.

Today, western scientists have come to see that men are not separate from nature, that things which appear to be separate from each other are not really so. Gradually, through the path of science, western people are working out the truth of Vedanta.

To India, Swamiji spoke in a different way. India had to put theory into practice. In theory, Indians knew that everything that existed was an expression of one Spirit, yet they did not carry this idea to its logical conclusion in everyday life. The logical conclusion would be that every aspect of life could serve as a means of reaching that one Spirit. Yet Indians had, unlike in their past, forgotten to harmonize material values with their spiritual heritage. They had lost all enthusiasm for everyday life.

Now the time had come, Swamiji told them, when they must imbibe from the West the spirit of enthusiasm and the desire to improve themselves. They must also learn science and technology from the West and build India up into a modern nation. But all this they must do only on the basis of Vedanta. Although Vedanta was a universal truth, of equal importance to all people, it was also India's own national ideal, and India must therefore practise it and teach it to others.

Swamiji foresaw the great interchange between East and West that is taking place at the present time. This interchange would lead to a complete world civilization. Civilization, he said, would only be complete in the world when India gave to the world the marvels of spiritual things, and, in exchange, received from the world the marvels of modern science.

So if we want to sum up Swamiji's teachings in a few words, it is the message of world civilization based on Vedanta.

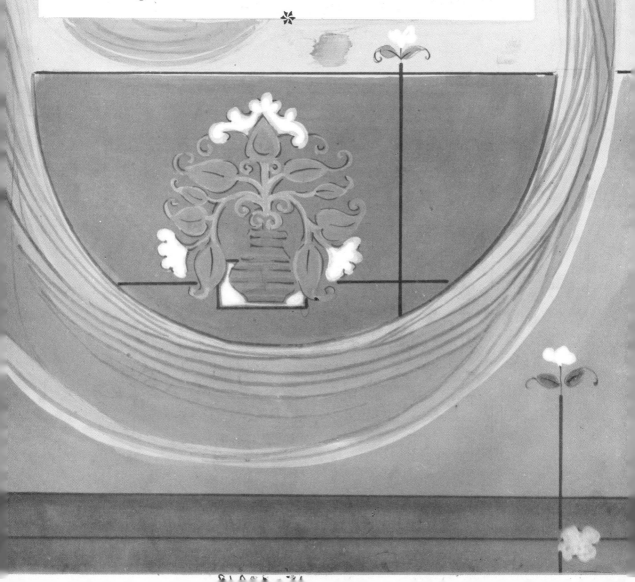

उत्तिष्ठत जाग्रत प्राप्य वरान्निबोधत

Arise! Awake! And Stop not
Till the Goal is Reached.